THE LIT
FLY F
TIPS

MICHAEL DEVENISH

THE LITTLE BOOK OF FLY FISHING TIPS

MICHAEL DEVENISH

A.
Absolute Press

First published in Great Britain in 2012 by
Absolute Press, an imprint of Bloomsbury Publishing Plc
Scarborough House, 29 James Street West
Bath BA1 2BT, England
Phone +44 (0)1225 316013 **Fax** +44 (0)1225 445836
E-mail info@absolutepress.co.uk
Web www.absolutepress.co.uk

A catalogue record of this book is available from the British Library
ISBN 13: 9781906650650
Printed and bound in Malta on behalf of Latitude Press

Bloomsbury Publishing Plc
50 Bedford Square, London WC1B 3DP | www.bloomsbury.com

'The jealous trout, that low did lie
Rose at a well dissembled fly'

**Isaac Walton quoting Sir Henry Wotton
in The Compleat Angler 1654**

1

Fly fishing is unlike all other methods of catching fish in that the ability to cast the fly line is essential before even contemplating fishing so if you are new to the art take a course from a pro

and **learn to cast.**

The few hours spent learning this skill correctly will avoid many more of frustration.

2

A floppy wrist will give a bad cast. Try to imagine that the rod is strapped to your arm and

keep your **wrist, forearm and rod in a straight line** then

imagine that you are hammering in a nail with a hammer. The rod will do the work for you.

3

We are usually taught that **during casting** the rod should work between 10 and 2 on the clock face. Start the cast between 11 and 1 and work towards 9.30 to 2.30 before shooting out the line. This compensates for the increasing line length in the air.

4

Many bad casts are caused by failing to let the back cast straighten out properly before pulling forward again. Try to **look over your shoulder** and see what is going on with the loop of line behind you **until you are able to cast** more instinctively.

5

A good quality rod that is comfortable to cast for hours at a time is very important so

when buying a fly rod always try to test it

out before you purchase or try a friend's rod and, if it suits you, only then should you look for a mail order bargain. Nearly all anglers have at least one rod they regret ever buying.

6

Rods range from 7ft 6in for small streams up to 12 feet or more for deep-water drift fishing and salmon. A mid-flex rod of 9 feet and weighing 3.5 to 4 ounces with an AFTM rating #6 is

a great place to start for a trout rod.

It will cover most situations from small still water lakes to streams and rivers.

7

Whatever rod, reel and line combination you opt for will depend on your personal circumstances. The reel only acts as a reservoir for the line so the most important point is that the

line and rod must be matched to **the same AFTM**

rating standard. AFTM stands for Association of Fishing Tackle Manufacturers and the higher the number the heavier the line and rod.
Do not mix and match AFTM numbers, it doesn't work.

8

Fly lines are also **rated according to their profile**

so alongside the AFTM rating will appear letters such as F (floating), S (sinking), WF (weight forward), DT (double taper) and so on. An understanding of these ratings is important and your tackle dealer will be happy to explain the nuances.

9

A floating fly line (F) will cover 80 per cent of most fly-fishing situations. It will allow you to fish entirely on the surface or with a long leader and weighted fly down to a depth of 4–5 feet which at most times of year will get you amongst the fish.

The floating line should always **be first choice for the beginner.**

10

Walk down **to the waterside with stealth** and discretion. The fish will see you silhouetted against the sky or feel you coming with their acute lateral senses long before you arrive and they won't be waiting for you to tackle up!

11

The standard Environment Agency fishing license will cover you for non-migratory trout but if you intend **to fish for salmon** or migratory sea trout **you** will **need a different license.**

12

Weather is important as trout and salmon do not like bright sunny days or warm water. Look for a cool-to-warm but overcast day with a gentle breeze if you are on a still water and without the breeze on the river for some of the best conditions to catch them.

13

Don't be bewildered by the fly catalogues. There are many hundreds of patterns available for differing situations yet most fly fishermen will admit to about a dozen or so

favourite fly patterns which they will use fairly consistently. More important is to try and learn how to 'match the hatch' and look in your fly box for a good approximation of what you think the trout are eating today.

Many professional entomologists are very good fly fishermen for this reason.

14

Fly is now a generic **term for any food source that can be imitated**

by tying fur and feather onto a hook and casting it with a fly rod. True flies are the various growth stages of caddisflies, damsels, dragonflies, mayflies, midges and stoneflies but terrestial insects such as grasshoppers, ants and caterpillars can all be imitated as well as crustaceans such as crabs and crayfish. All are important to a fish's diet and all can be represented in your fly box.

15

If you are fishing a river **try casting into the pools** downstream from any water which has run over shallows or waterfalls and rocks. These areas of water will contain the most saturated oxygen and will attract fish to them for that reason.

16

The length of monofilament **trace attached to** the tip of **the fly line** onto which your fly or flies are tied **is called the leader.** This can be anything from six to twelve feet long and should also be tapered down to the tip to help the presentation of the fly as it lands on the water. Leaders are easily made up using simple knots and graduating thicknesses of monofilament.

17

When tying up leaders for deeper water fishing a 5–6 inch length of line left at each joining knot will enable another fly to be attached. This is called

a dropper and leaving

in two along the length of the leader

will enable three flies to be fished

simultaneously as a team. On streams it's best to stick with a single fly.

18

Fly Fishing Knots Tip #1

Your fly line will be attached to perhaps thirty to forty yards of backing line which will sit on the reel spindle or arbor. This backing line is attached to the fly reel spindle with an

Arbor Knot.

19

Fly Fishing Knots Tip #2

The fly line is traditionally attached to the backing line with a needle knot but as this is a tricky knot to do well a good alternative and my personal preference) is the

Albright knot

which is just as durable when tied well and finished off with a small drop of superglue.

20

Fly Fishing Knots Tip #3

To attach the leader to the fly line a very helpful modern innovation is the

braided nylon tube loop system. These braided loops fit over the fly line and pull on very tightly. Properly used with a sleeve and finished again with a drop of superglue these loops are a great replacement for a knot.

21

Fly Fishing Knots Tip #4

The best knot to use when tying your fly onto the leader is the **tucked blood knot or clinch knot** but whatever you choose to call it, always use an absolute minimum of six turns onto the body of the line before locking up the knot. Nothing less will do.

22

Fly Fishing Knots Tip #5

For making up leaders by joining lengths of monofilament, the easiest knot to use is the **water knot.** The **full blood knot** and the **double grinner knot** are better if you intend to leave in droppers to carry extra flies on the leader.

23

Fly Fishing Knots Tip #6

Whenever tying knots in monofilament

always lubricate the knot

before tightening it up. Vegetable oil is best, saliva is far more commonly used. Monofilament can lose up to fifty per cent of its breaking strength at the knot so avoiding the heat caused by friction when tightening up is essential.

24

The retrieve is the art of pulling one's fly back towards you to imitate the natural moving fly through the water.

There are various methods of retrieving the fly

for different circumstances, but all depend crucially upon avoiding slack in the fly line as much as possible. The straightest line in the circumstances is always best in order to set the hook on a bite.

25

When lifting the fly off the water

at the end of a retrieve, lift the rod gently and try to wait until you can see the fly and make sure it is not being followed. A curious trout will often pursue the fly right up until the last moment and if the fish doesn't see you first and bolt anyway he will be forced to make a decision or lose a meal as the fly leaves the water.

26

Salmon and trout have hard bony mouths and that can make it difficult to set a hook so get a good hook file and **always keep your hooks sharp.**

It will make all the difference.

27

If you intend to return your fish to the water after capture then flatten down the barb on the hook before using it.

A barbless hook is much **easier to remove safely**

from the fish and will minimise damage.

28

Do your best to avoid handling a fish if you intend to release it again. The slime coat on a fish is very important to its ability to withstand damage and disease. Much better to wet your hands and try **to unhook the fish in the water** using forceps or small pliers to remove the hook.

29

If it has fought well before capture your fish will be exhausted. Returned in this condition it will probably not have the strength left to stay upright and will roll over and die. If you intend to release it hold the fish upright around the 'wrist' where the tail connects to the body and rock it gently to and fro in the water for a few minutes. This will pass water and air over the gills and

allow the fish to recover.

Let it go when it feels ready.

30

Fishing a deep reservoir

in early season

especially from a boat is when you will usually

need to **fish deep**

and slow

using a sinking line. Sinking fly lines can be slow-, medium- or fast-sinking or even lead-cored for super-fast-sinking. They cast differently from the usual floating line so practice before you go.

31

Rainbow trout stocked into lakes and reservoirs tend to **shoal up** and stay that way meaning good fishing when you locate the shoal.

The English native **brown trout is more solitary** and territorial and will be harder to find. The margins and around sunken obstacles are good places to start looking.

32

If you do use a landing net make sure that it is a modern knotless version, anything else is illegal. Be sure to get the net fully submerged into the the water well before the fish is near.

Many fish are lost through being spooked **at the last moment** by a net splashing into the water.

33

The fly fisherman does not need boxes and boxes of tackle at the waterside and for that reason can remain highly mobile.

A good waistcoat style **fishing vest** with multiple pockets **is all you need** to carry everything required to fish and is a worthy investment.

34

A wide-brimmed **hat will** not only **protect you** from the sun but is also a good safety measure when fly fishing. A badly cast fly (and we all do it occasionally) is better caught in your hat than in your face or eye.

35

When fishing upstream in a river keep the line short

and retrieve at the speed of the current to appear as natural as possible. Remember also that the fish will almost certainly be facing away from you with its head into the current so watch your shadow and move slowly and carefully.

36

When fishing downstream in a river, **cast across the current** and follow your fly downstream with the rod tip to increase your chances. Also remember that the fish will be facing you now so always move slowly and carefully.

37

Getting in the river is always **fun** and will increase your chances **but wading can be dangerous**

so always use a flotation collar. In the water, move diagonally across the current, and using a shuffle-type step always keep both feet on the ground.

38

Fullers earth paste is used to coat the leader and get it to break through the surface of the water and sink. This enables your flies to be fished much more discreetly without leaving a leader trail in the surface. When you finish fishing **add water to your fullers earth** pot then shake it out and seal it up. This will avoid it drying out and it will be in perfect condition next time you need it.

39

Many hours of standing by water will expose you to a lot of surface glare which can cause headaches and sunburn. A pair of

polarised sun glasses are essential to cut through this surface glare and will also enable you to see right into the water and spot the fish before they spot you.

40

It might seem obvious but fishing rods and lightning don't mix. **A carbon fishing rod is a lightning conductor,** so sit out the storm and keep safe. Also watch out for high-voltage overhead cables and do not cast anywhere near them.

41

Sunny days by the water will require the use of sun block but even the merest hint of this chemical concoction in the water will put the fish off, so always **wash your hands after applying sun block** and before handling flies and leaders.

42

Fly lines are expensive so they **need protecting** from contact with liquids such as sun block, insect repellent and fuel. Clean your lines regularly using only mild soap and clean water and re-plasticise the line annually with line plasticizer.

43

When we talk about fly fishing we usually think trout and sometimes salmon.

Other UK fish that will take a fly include Pike, Carp and Grayling whilst Sea Bass on the coast will also oblige. Adjustments will need to be made to tackle but the principle is exactly the same.

44

Fly fishing tackle and in particular multi-piece travelling rods have improved hugely in recent years such that the list of species that can be caught on a fly rod is now extensive so why not

try a foreign fly fishing holiday.

From largemouth bass in America to bonefish in Cuba via Taimen in Mongolia and dozens more international species – the world is your oyster.

45

Looking good in the fly box for an artificial is only the beginning. **Your fly** also **has to look alive and natural** in the water.

The depth fished at and the style of retrieve is often more important than the choice of fly. A fish has to believe that your artificial offering is alive and trying to escape from its hungry jaws so think like an insect.

46

Try casting a small fish fry imitator into the margins of still waters in the Autumn.

When the fish are feeding up in late Summer

to pack on the weight for Winter they will often come right into the shallows to gorge on small baitfish. This is often called fry bashing and a fast retrieved silver imitation can produce spectacular results.

47

When fishing a sinking line

in deep water

a good way to judge depth is to

count down as your fly sinks.

This will allow you to accurately fish all depths and find the bottom but more importantly will enable you to get back to the correct depth once you locate the fish.

48

Another obvious tip often forgotten **when fly fishing in the sea** is very important to the health of your tackle. Always remember to **rinse all tackle in fresh water after use.** Salt water is very corrosive especially to reels and flies.

49

If you are fishing for the table and intend **to kill a fish** then do it properly and immediately using a Priest. This is a heavy instrument used to **hit** the fish **smartly on the back of its head.** 'Administering the last rites' by using a priest is the best way to despatch fish quickly and humanely.

50

A clothing essential for fly fishermen happy to brave colder weather in the early season is

fingerless neoprene gloves. These will **keep your hands warm** whilst, more importantly, still allowing proper control of the fly line.

Michael Devenish

Michael Devenish wasted much of the first fifty years of his angling life being a successful businessman and mortgage payer. From childhood messing in streams and ponds to fly fishing for trout, his piscatorial horizons gradually expanded to include coarse and sea fishing throughout the UK along with regular expeditions to the remote jungle rivers of the Amazon basin in search of exotic and predatory species. He has also fished extensively in India, Africa and Central America. At home in the south-west of England he keeps koi carp in his garden pond and stocks and runs a small trout lake with friends.

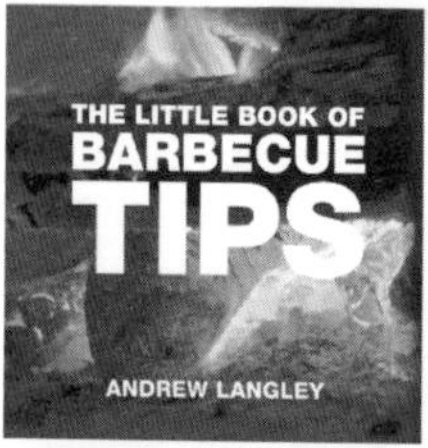
THE LITTLE BOOK OF
BARBECUE
TIPS
ANDREW LANGLEY

THE LITTLE BOOK OF
BEER
TIPS
ANDREW LANGLEY
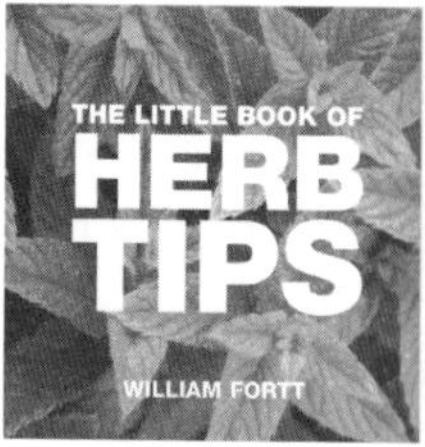
THE LITTLE BOOK OF
HERB
TIPS
WILLIAM FORTT

THE LITTLE BOOK OF
POKER
TIPS
PETER FRENCH
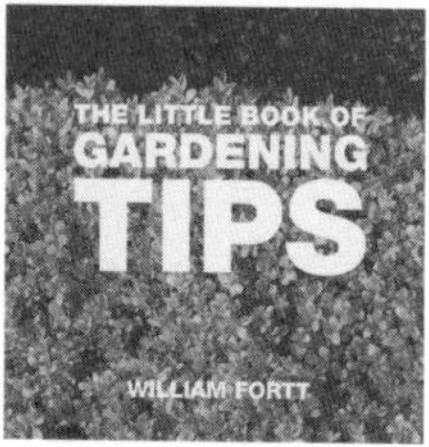
THE LITTLE BOOK OF
GARDENING
TIPS
WILLIAM FORTT

THE LITTLE BOOK OF
CHEFS'
TIPS
RICHARD MAGGS

THE LITTLE BOOK OF
SPICE
TIPS
ANDREW LANGLEY

THE LITTLE BOOK OF
GOLF
TIPS
PETER FRENCH

THE LITTLE BOOK OF
TIPS
SERIES

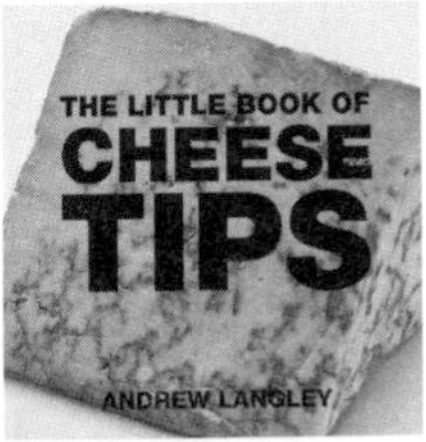
THE LITTLE BOOK OF
CHEESE
TIPS
ANDREW LANGLEY

THE LITTLE BOOK OF
WINE
TIPS
ANDREW LANGLEY

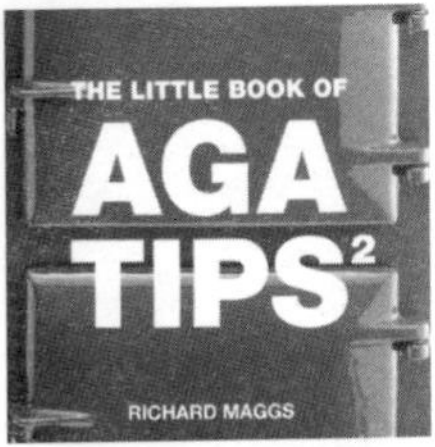
THE LITTLE BOOK OF
AGA
TIPS²
RICHARD MAGGS

THE LITTLE BOOK OF
COFFEE
TIPS
ANDREW LANGLEY

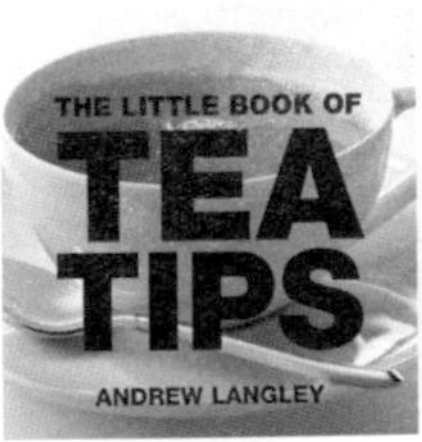
THE LITTLE BOOK OF
TEA
TIPS
ANDREW LANGLEY

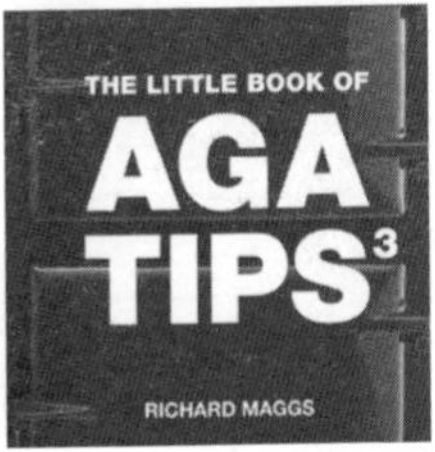
THE LITTLE BOOK OF
AGA
TIPS³
RICHARD MAGGS

THE LITTLE BOOK OF
AGA
TIPS
RICHARD MAGGS

THE LITTLE BOOK OF
CHRISTMAS
AGA
TIPS
RICHARD MAGGS

THE LITTLE BOOK OF
RAYBURN
TIPS
RICHARD MAGGS

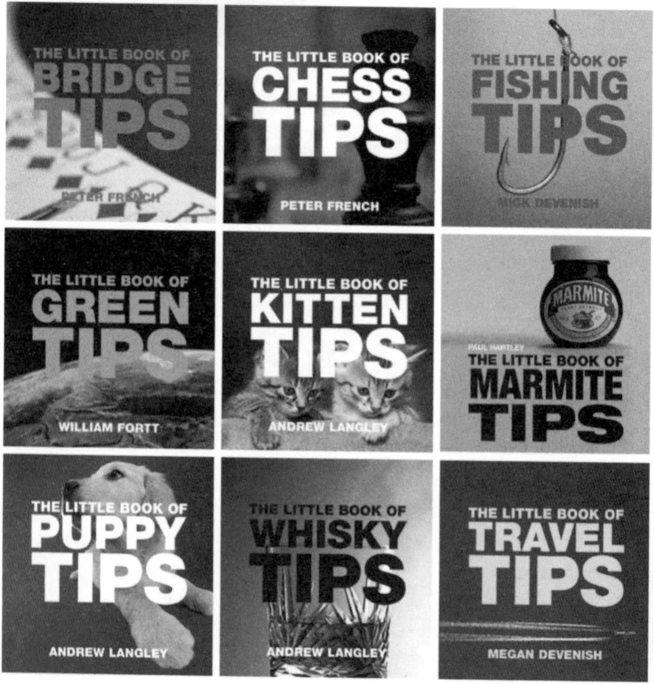
THE LITTLE BOOK OF
BRIDGE
TIPS
PETER FRENCH
THE LITTLE BOOK OF
CHESS
TIPS
PETER FRENCH
THE LITTLE BOOK OF
FISHING
TIPS
MICK DEVENISH
THE LITTLE BOOK OF
GREEN
TIPS
WILLIAM FORTT
THE LITTLE BOOK OF
KITTEN
TIPS
ANDREW LANGLEY
MARMITE
PAUL HARTLEY
THE LITTLE BOOK OF
MARMITE
TIPS
THE LITTLE BOOK OF
PUPPY
TIPS
ANDREW LANGLEY
THE LITTLE BOOK OF
WHISKY
TIPS
ANDREW LANGLEY
THE LITTLE BOOK OF
TRAVEL
TIPS
MEGAN DEVENISH